Sacredly Profane

Also by Kevin Densley
Vigorous Vernacular (Picaro Press)
Lionheart Summer (Picaro Press)
Orpheus in the Undershirt (Ginninderra Press)

Kevin Densley

Sacredly Profane

Acknowledgements

Poems in this collection have been published, sometimes in slightly different form, in the following journals: *Azuria, foam:e, The Footy Almanac, The Journal* (UK), *Nightingale & Sparrow* (USA), *Orbis* (UK), *Quadrant, Sage Cigarettes, Southerly, tamba* and *The Wellington Street Review* (UK).
'Caspar David' was anthologised in *Mountain Secrets* (Ginninderra Press, 2019).
Thanks to the editors of these publications.

Sacredly Profane
ISBN 978 1 76109 032 5
Copyright © Kevin Densley 2020
Cover art: Julian Di Martino

First published 2020 by
GINNINDERRA PRESS
PO Box 3461 Port Adelaide 5015
www.ginninderrapress.com.au

Contents

The Day I Broke Billy	7
Thumbnail Sketch of the Great Roy Orbison	8
The 'Vision' Thing	9
Sea Horse	11
Painterly	12
House by the Sea	13
Sundays in Geelong	14
Cracker Night	15
From Lemprière's Dictionary	16
The Local Mayor Launches a Literary Magazine at the Outer Suburban Campus of a Large University	17
Kitchen	21
Deptford, London, 30 May 1593	22
Near Drowning at St Leonard's Beach, Victoria, 1967	23
Wednesday Evening, St Matthew's Anglican Church, East Geelong	24
From Sheffield, England	25
In the Manner of C.P.E. Bach	26
Vienna Dream	27
The Quest of the Holy Grail – in a Nutshell	29
Bert Watts's Pies	30
Uncle Bert and the 1909 Melbourne to Warrnambool Cycling Race	31
Wedding Party Photograph: the Marriage of Lucy Jane R– to Edward Thomas P–, the town of P–, South Australia, 20 December 1905	32
Irish	36
Sorrento, Victoria, 1983	37
Mirror	38
Muscular Christianity	39

In a Kelly town museum	40
Platinum Blonde	41
Pink Rose, Framed by a Window	42
Bad Behaviour	43
Hieronymus Bosch's *The Conjuror* (c. 1502)	44
Bushranger Jimmy Governor, Hanged, Darlinghurst Jail, 18 January 1901	45
To Leanne, My Long-lost Friend, Nude in Last Night's Dream	46
4 Carrington Street	47
Fighting Words	48
Photograph of Multiple Murderer and Bushranger Tommy Clarke of the Notorious Braidwood Clarkes Aboard the Stolen Racehorse Boomerang, circa 1865	49
Beyond Goyder's Line, South Australia	50
After Reading Ovid's Daedalus	51
Ned Kelly's Last Hours	52
Bob Craig's Funeral	53
The Capture and Incarceration of Frank 'Captain Melville' McCallum (1822–1857)	54
Stringybark Creek	58
Self-portrait with Death Playing the Fiddle	59
Caspar David	60
The Great War – AIF Suite	61

The Day I Broke Billy

The day I broke Billy,
the stadium (well, athletics track)
was cool, windless.
The 800 metres final.
Young William was my rival.
Nerves, muscles and tendons attenuated,
we gathered at the starting line.
The gun cracked
– I led. Felt good.
The tartan flew beneath my feet.
Bill tracked my every step. I could
sense his determination.
His father had perched himself on the fence
at the end of lap one,
where Bill had planned
to make a drawn-out finishing kick.
(I knew his tactics of old.)
A bloke in a long grey coat rang the bell.
Bill's dad let out a rousing yell,
'C'mon, Billy!'
I still felt strong, upped the pace,
while Bill let out a guttural cry
'I c-c-c-can't!'
in response to his father's call.
That was all I needed.
I sped, unchallenged, to the finish line,
then turned and watched those in my wake.
Bill lolloped like a busted tyre
into second place,
on that special day in the Under Elevens
when I shattered him like a meringue.

Thumbnail Sketch of the Great Roy Orbison

Mellow, honeyed voice
in that lilting, Southern boy style.
Range encompassing octaves.

Got taught to ride motorcycles
by his good friend,
Elvis the King.

Thank ya very much, ladies un gennlemen.
Thank ya very much.
Thank ya very much, sayhd Elhvus.

Wella wella wella,
bless my soul,
what wrong with me? sang Elhvus.

As a kid I thought Roy was blind
because he wore
those trademark big dark glasses…

he died too young,
had a heart attack
one winter night,

after flying model aeroplanes
with his young kids.

The 'Vision' Thing

(George Bush Sr during the 1992 US presidential campaign)

George Bush sat glumly in a room
in the West Wing of the White House
surrounded by concerned advisors.
He'd just had his butt kicked
on nationwide TV
in the Richmond debate
by Bill Clinton. (There were times when,
seemingly unaware of the cameras,
he actually took a peek at his watch,
as if anxious for the whole ordeal
to be over
– he didn't appear that interested
in what was being discussed at the time;
namely, the nation's future.)
'Mr President,' said one of the staffers
in the West Wing room,
snapping him out of his abstraction,
'There is a perception, however wrong,
that you have no major plans
for the next four years
if re-elected.
You need to tell the people
what you are going to do,
not only what you've done for them
up until now.'

'Oh yeah,' the President replied,
his mind beginning to drift again,
as he gazed through the wide bay windows
at two dogs (Pekinese, he thought)
fucking on the lawn.
'Yeah, Bob. That's it
– the "vision" thing.'

Sea Horse

Phosphorescent,
membranous,
delicate as an embryo,
the sea horse we netted from the pier
when we were ten-year-old boys.
We took it to an aquarium.
A man there gladly received this glittery
resident of the bay
and placed it in salt water,
temperature-controlled.
We watched for a while through glass.
But soon, moonstone-eerie,
all lights going out,
it sank to the bottom,
too precious to live.

Painterly

Titian light
filled the backyard
near sunset, after the thunderstorm

as if an ancient deity
had roused from aeonian sleep
then tinted the air.

House by the Sea

Why, across years, decades, does my mind keep returning to an old weatherboard house by the sea in winter? To white-capped, deep blue waves, on the other side of nearby dunes, seen through the glass of a slightly open window? A curtain turning and tossing in a fluky wind? What about the cracks in the plaster of this room's walls and ceiling? The antique black-and-white TV in the corner, switched off, it seems, forever? And the yellowed wallpaper dotted with tiny pink flowers? The dusty coffee table with a cut-glass vase in the centre, upon a once-white lace doily? The creaking timber of the house's frame, the high-pitched grinding of the sheets of the corrugated-iron roof? Why am I suddenly, palpably there, *here*, wondering why I'm present?

Sundays in Geelong

Sundays were family days, with my father, mother, two younger sisters. Morning mass at St Mary's, then fish and chips at Eastern Beach, sharp salt smell of the bay, whiff of rotting seaweed, feeding the leftovers to brawling seagulls. A visit to my grandmother's: a cup of tea and love. Afternoons watching VFA football on black-and-white TV, spaghetti for tea (Kookaburra No. 2 tubular), topped with canned Campbell's sauce. A half-interesting documentary after the 6 p.m. news about Victoria's shipwreck coast, voiced with reassuring calm by newsreader, Brian Naylor, many years later to die with his wife in the flames of the Kinglake bushfires.

Cracker Night

(the sale of fireworks was outlawed in Victoria in 1982)

What a shame
we can no longer
celebrate Guy Fawkes night:
build a fiery mountain
in our backyard;
set off penny bangers,
skyrockets and jumping jacks;
make a letter box explode;
blind a mate in the eye;
blow off one of our fingers.

From Lemprière's Dictionary

In the beginning,
Chaos,
the world nothing
but 'a rude and shapeless
mass of matter',
according to Lemprière,
a poet in his way.

The Local Mayor Launches a Literary Magazine at the Outer Suburban Campus of a Large University

He is the local mayor
– cheap-suited, red-faced,
in his late forties, the type
who'd rort his travel expenses,
be having it off with his secretary,
give inside knowledge
of council zoning decisions
to disreputable business mates
and happily cook the books
of his chain of hardware stores.
But he acts like the proverbial pie
at this literary launch.
You can tell he'd prefer not to be here,
under this marquee,
with academics, students
and a couple of guest poets.

'What the fuck do I know
about launching a poetry magazine?
Can't someone else do it?'
he asked his deputy,
a few days earlier.
'No. It has to be you.
Some of the uni's top brass will be there.
They've asked for the mayor and want to be seen
to be' (he does the inverted commas fingers)
'"fostering links with the local community".'

'Those eggheads couldn't give a fuck either,'
replied the mayor.
'I know those types.
On big salaries, good perks.
Do bugger all.
All right, I suppose I'll have to go.
Might take some heat off me...
that shit they've been writing
in the local rag
– I gave that contract to my brother
because he supplied the best tender.'
'I know, I know,' the deputy replied.
'Want a cappuccino, boss?
I'm just nicking out.'
'No, mate. Thanks.'

Back at the launch,
the mayor is at the microphone,
sweating and smiling.
Holding the poetry mag in his hands,
he says, as if making a point
of considerable importance,
'You call this a magazine. I call it a book.
I don't know why you say *magazine*.
It's definitely a book to me.'
Most of his audience stare blankly, bored.
The uni's top brass chuckle
at the mayor's sad attempt at humour.
'I was a bit of a writer once myself...'
(or some such crap).

He is right
– they don't really care
about what is going on.
To them, this occasion is merely
an item to be noted
in their annual report:
yearly production of lit magazine – check.
Me? I am sniffing
the sausages spitting on the barbecue,
lamenting the occasion is dry.
New campus regulations have declared
the uni alcohol-free,
except for high-level board meetings
and occasions deemed important
by the vice-chancellor (or his representative)
– this one doesn't qualify.
Icy wind howls across the campus.
Light rain starts to fall.
Bill and I, the guest poets,
read our inclusions in the mag
to a smattering of polite applause.
I eat three sausages in bread
and two egg-and-lettuce sandwiches
but don't have the money
to join the students later for a drink.
The rain starts down in bucketloads
as I run for my car,
one kilometre away
to avoid the campus parking costs.

I drive off, soaking wet,
wondering as I pass
seemingly endless kilometres
of a desert that's outer suburbia
– was it worth going there at all?

Kitchen

Cod is battered.
Lamb hammered.
Vegetables knifed
into pieces.

Chickens skewered.
Carcasses stripped.
Crustaceans boiled,
dismembered.

Garlic crushed.
Strawberries pulped.

Even the concrete floor
is distressed.

Deptford, London, 30 May 1593

Near sunset. A dank,
low-ceilinged room
in the house of Mrs Bull.
You can feel the damp rising.
Old Father Thames laps
the muddy banks outside.
Four men dine in a private suite,
their conversation quiet, intense.
Then an eruption,
a full-blown fight,
over the *recknynge*.
Marlowe the playwright lashes at Frizer,
having snatched the latter's dagger.
Frizer wrestles the weapon back
and stabs the playwright above the right eye.
With a wound two inches deep,
Marlowe slumps and dies.
Frizer is imprisoned,
but soon found innocent.
Self-defence is not a crime.

Near Drowning at St Leonard's Beach, Victoria, 1967

Nearly drowned
when I was five.
My father saved my life.
Was paddling at St Leonard's beach,
not far from shore,
when I stepped into a pothole
and was suddenly out of my depth.
Couldn't swim.
Went down once.
Struggled to the surface.
Twice.
Battled up again,
to glimpse my father,
sprinting, splashing towards me.
Had gone down for a third time,
when I felt his powerful hands
take me under the armpits
and snatch me from oblivion.
My father and I have never talked freely;
we've certainly not discussed
the time he saved my life.
And never will.

Wednesday Evening, St Matthew's Anglican Church, East Geelong

One night a week, as a child,
returning home from my grandparents'
in the family car,
I'd pass this dark brick church,
its yellow stained-glass windows
blooming with holy light.

Sometimes, with my window down,
glorious Evensong voices
were carried to me by the wind.

From Sheffield, England

In Australia, many of our grandparents
got Viner and Hall cutlery
– the really good stuff –
for wedding presents.
Often they passed it on.
Look in your kitchen drawers;
examine the knives, forks and spoons.
Your past may be in your hands.

In the Manner of C.P.E. Bach

Not
in the style of
Johann Sebastian,
nor Johann Christian, 'the London Bach',
and definitely not the way
that the restless and dissatisfied
Wilhelm Friedemann Bach might have played it,
no –
play it for me
in the manner of 'the Hamburg Bach',
Carl Philipp Emmanuel.

Vienna Dream

It's 1825.
I'm in a Viennese coffee house,
at a window table,
gazing at the snow-lined street.
A stern-looking, grey-haired man bustles past
in a fur coat, thumping his gloved hands together.
In the freezing cold, his breath comes out
as puffs of steam.
'Herr Beethoven!' a man cries out,
and frantically waves from across the road
but he does not hear the greeting, of course,
and soon disappears from my sight.
Over in the corner
of the room I'm sitting in,
past the heavy, exquisitely carved,
darkly varnished tables and chairs,
a pudgy, bespectacled man, quite young,
is seated at a piano.
He's surrounded by some well-dressed males,
obviously his friends.
They laugh, converse and drink beer
with considerable bonhomie.
Then all is suddenly quiet
as the man in the glasses begins to play.
The glorious tenor voice
of one of the company joins in,
filling the room with a melody
as beautiful and sad as unrequited love.
I raise my mug of steaming coffee
and savour the smell of the cinnamon.

I take a sip, and listen, in thrall.
I *have* to introduce myself, I think,
to the one who composed this wonderful song!
At its conclusion, I leave my table
and walk across the room.
The young man at the piano
has turned around.
He looks directly at me
with a quizzical expression.
I smile, and offer my hand:
'Herr Schubert, I…'

The Quest of the Holy Grail – in a Nutshell

The country has fallen into wickedness.
Arthur, its king,
sends a group of knights
on a quest to obtain a wonderful thing,
a Holy Grail that will rid the place
of its grave afflictions
– crops will once again flourish,
people will resume being good,
et cetera, et cetera.
By way of their flaws,
most knights fail.
Except for a few;
one, Galahad,
a Christlike figure,
too good to be true;
another, Lancelot, flawed carnally
– in that respect, at least,
a credible human being.
After years of battles, prophesying monks
and much multilevel symbolism,
the successful questers obtain a vision
of the wonderful Grail.
But God doesn't let them have it:
the country is too sinful to be saved
and it's taken to another land.

Colossal letdown.

Bert Watts's Pies

As young men in Millicent, South Australia,
my grandfather and his mates
went on the occasional bender.
After such occasions, when he woke up crook
and had to face his mother,
a formidable woman of German stock,
he always blamed Bert Watts,
the local pastry cook.
'It must have been Bert Watts's pies,'
he said to his mum, who did not believe him
but didn't let on. She figured
he was a good boy, and young men
did this sort of thing.
Many years later, my father
used a similar excuse with my mother.
Often, on summer nights,
when afternoon shift
at the refinery had ended,
a group of the blokes would cross the road
and cook a barbecue on the beach.
Cold amber ales were plentiful.
Though not a big drinker,
sometimes my father would have his share.
When he'd get home to my mother,
worse for wear, he'd say,
'It must have been the sausages.'
She was awake up to him, too,
but, like my great-grandmother,
let it go through to the 'keeper.

Uncle Bert and the 1909 Melbourne to Warrnambool Cycling Race

Uncle Bert and my great-grandfather, Fardie,
rode in the 1909
Melbourne to Warrnambool wheel race.
Near Stony Rises, three-quarters through
the 120-mile journey,
Uncle Bert hit a fox terrier
and went arse over proverbial.
My grandfather, Fardie's son,
told me this yarn and recalled
how Bert was picking pebbles
out of his knees for the following week.
What happened to the errant dog
remained unsaid.

Wedding Party Photograph: the Marriage of Lucy Jane R– to Edward Thomas P–, the town of P–, South Australia, 20 December 1905

Henry R–,
my great-great grandfather,
farmer, publican,
world traveller,
looks a million pounds,
immaculately groomed
in his stylish suit,
smiling, bow tie,
flower in lapel,
fob watch nestled in pocket.
Next, his wife, Mary Jane,
slender, serious,
wears a striking long dress
patterned with circular shapes.
Its dominant colour?
Dark blue? Chartreuse?
No way of telling in black-and-white.
Did she buy the dress in Paris
when her and Henry
attended the Exposition?

Then great-great Aunt Martha P–,
destined for spinsterhood,
slump-shouldered and glum
next to her brother,
great-great Uncle Billy,
with his sad droopy moustache.
He spent much of the First World War,
judging by his army record,
giving cheek to his superiors.

Next to him is the bride,
Lucy, my great-grandmother,
daughter of Henry and Mary Jane,
pretty, dark-haired, innocent-eyed,
seven decades younger
than the shrunken ninety-year-old I knew
in the country hospital dementia ward.
Then, of course, the groom,
my great-grandfather, Ted,
who died before I was born,
showing the camera
a smug expression;
spoon player, ballroom dancer,
billiard parlour owner.

Then fourteen-year-old Maud,
my great-grandmother's sister,
pianist and singer;
highly strung and eccentric,
according to family tradition.
She's holding an enormous bouquet.
Two years before, played a silver-winged fairy
in her school pageant.
Three years later was married,
giving birth to her first child.
A dozen more years and four more kids,
till one day she left her marital home
with the youngest and a suitcase
that she could barely carry.
Next, her brother Fred, aged twenty,
dapper like his father,
married and running a pub
in red dust near the Goyder line
within two years.

After Fred, Bridget,
my Irish great-great-grandmother,
smiling, a big woman, motherly.
With Bridget,
great-great grandfather William,
the local ranger, well-known breeder
of prize-winning hens and roosters.
His suit does not fit well,
he isn't wearing a tie
and his shoes could do with a polish.

Finally, in the front,
flower girl Ella,
smiling sweetly, an intelligent face;
niece of Nathaniel B–,
the greatest footballer
to pull on a boot in the town's history.
Nat MC'd the dances
held in the Institute Hall;
indeed, he did likewise
at this wedding reception.
He died twenty-two years later
from a heart attack while discussing
the fortunes of the local team.
He thought he had indigestion.

Irish

Through centuries
we've roved and raved
around the world,
and time,
ceaseless snow,
falls faintly
and faintly falls:
we are one,
we are one.
We are still one.

Sorrento, Victoria, 1983

A distant summer day,
spent with my girlfriend-at-the-time
– the ferry ride
where we saw no dolphins,
supposed to be a highlight of the trip
– the maritime museum
where all I remember
was a yellowed newspaper clipping,
tacked behind glass,
about a man who went to the beach,
decades before;
football star, strong swimmer,
he disappeared beneath the waves
while his wife and kids on shore looked on.
He was taken by a shark,
randomly snatched
from frolicking and laughter
– and the ridiculously fashionable
salmon pink shirt I wore,
patterned with geometric
lime green and sky blue shapes.
My girlfriend-at-the-time,
a fashion design student,
bought it for my birthday.

This happened an aeon ago.
My girlfriend-at-the-time and I
soon separated, painfully.
A decade later, she hanged herself.

Mirror

A pattern
in the bark of a tree
becomes a human face
– totemic, wild, sad.
I blink.

The face has disappeared.

Muscular Christianity

Looking at the Station of the Cross
in which Christ is stripped, I reflect
– He must have been working out.
(Check out that six-pack gut!)
But who was His personal trainer?

God the Father?

In a Kelly town museum

near the bluestone step
on which Byrne

stuck a boot
as he gunned down

Sherritt, the mummified
conjoined heads

of a freak calf hang
upon a meat hook

Platinum Blonde

Jean Harlow
faded into
the background
of a gleaming black-and-white
Hollywood studio
glamour portrait,
late in the 1930s.
She disappeared
into a moody *mise-en-scène*,
didn't die aged twenty-six,
like the papers said.

Pink Rose, Framed by a Window

I like this title
so much
I'm content
to end the poem here.

Bad Behaviour

(Source: Harry Densley recounting an incident from his childhood in the *Ballan Times*, Victoria, 'Early Ballan. No. 5', by Jas. H. Walsh, 1/2/1917)

Van Diemen's Land, about 1848:
my four times great-grandfather, Thomas,
gave his young son, Harry
(brother of my three times great-grandfather, James),
a belting,
because he wagged school
to attend a triple public hanging
outside the Launceston Gaol.

Hieronymus Bosch's *The Conjuror* (c. 1502)

In Bosch's *The Conjuror*,
a rich merchant stares stupidly
at a magician performing a simple trick
while the magician's accomplice
picks the merchant's pocket.

Fools abound in every era,
asking, crying out
to be taken for a ride.

Bushranger Jimmy Governor, Hanged, Darlinghurst Jail, 18 January 1901

Jimmy Governor
was dropped on his arse
by a load of buckshot.

Doctors took
nearly fifty slugs
from his legs and back

so he could walk
with a steady gait
to the gallows.

To Leanne, My Long-lost Friend, Nude in Last Night's Dream

Leanne, my long-lost friend,
you were nude in last night's dream.
You slipped your slinky negligee
off your shoulders to the floor.
And there you stood,
all feminine curves,
beguiling, non-Brazilian.
You encouraged the rest of us in the room
to follow your startling lead.
Others quickly did so.
Nervously, I disrobed.
We intended to run out the door
and frolic in Arcady (I presume).
But we never got there.
Amid a blur
of pubic forests and naked skin,
alas my dream was over.

4 Carrington Street

In Aunty W's house – you could almost hear the wallpaper fading
In Aunty W's house – you could almost hear the faded
    wallpaper peeling off the wall
In Aunty W's house – the interior was dull, as musty as an attic

In Aunty W's house, unceasingly,
the smell of menthol cigarettes
wafted from her bedroom

Fighting Words

My father,
a former boxer,
only taught me one poem
– about an Australian World Bantamweight champ:

Lionel Rose
sat on a pin.

Lionel rose.

Photograph of Multiple Murderer and Bushranger Tommy Clarke of the Notorious Braidwood Clarkes Aboard the Stolen Racehorse Boomerang, circa 1865

According to a contemporary,
journalist Charles White,
the Clarke brothers, Tommy and John,
were of vicious stock.
He then offered evidence
from various parts of their family tree:
a father who died in jail,
under a charge of murder;
an uncle charged with being accessory
to the killing of a police party;
yet other uncles,
convicted highway robbers;
an aunt, a receiver of stolen goods…
anyway, here's a photograph
of Tommy, smiling,
easy in the saddle,
aboard a fleet-footed thoroughbred.
Just picture a crim of today
at the wheel of a Ferrari…

Beyond Goyder's Line, South Australia

Two nineteenth-century graves
in the red, sandy earth
of Johnburgh cemetery
– no headstones.
An old council plan
shows where they are buried:
William,
who died aged three years nine months
'after four hours' illness',
and Ethel,
who passed away at nine months
of 'teething and convulsions'.
Their parents, my great-great-grandfather, Henry,
and great-great-grandmother, Mary Jane,
farmed, and ran the pub nearby,
in the middle of nowhere.
Recently, when I phoned a local
and asked if any visible sign remained
of William and Ethel's graves
(being unable to travel there in person),
he answered,
'There is nothing but shifting sand.'

The quotes relating to William and Ethel's deaths come from contemporary South Australian newspaper death notices. Goyder's line concerns a line on a map drawn by South Australian Surveyor- General, George Goyder, in 1865, to separate – in his judgement – the arable area of the colony from the land unsuitable for crop growing and, therefore, any kind of intensive settlement. History has proved Goyder's line highly accurate – north of the line, further into the outback, there are many ghost towns, and all kinds of architectural ruins, where people tried and failed to make a living in the harsh environment.

After Reading Ovid's Daedalus

Daedalus, in the popular imagination, is a kindly old bloke, bearded, grey-haired, a bit of a whiz at inventing things – a bloody genius, really, to design that labyrinth. The story is widely known of how, to escape from Minos in Crete, he built wings for himself and Icarus his son. A good father, also, he warned the boy not to fly too high or the wax would run like oil and he'd plunge into the sea, which of course is what the stupid kid did – teenagers are so irresponsible. Sad and broken, Daedalus reached Sicily, where he saw a talking partridge that reminded him of a terrible crime he'd committed back in Athens: in a fit of jealous rage, he murdered his clever twelve-year-old nephew by throwing him down a flight of stairs. Decidedly *not* the action, I'm sure we'd all agree, of a fuzzy, warm old guy.

Ned Kelly's Last Hours

On his last night,
Kelly slept fitfully
after a final meal
of roast lamb and peas
washed down with a bottle of claret.
He rose at five a.m.,
prayed,
sang some bush ballads
then briefly went back to sleep.
At eight a.m., he walked
across the prison yard
toward his place of execution,
remarked upon the beauty of some flowers,
saw the dray for his dead body.
At ten a.m., upon the gallows,
the petty thief Upjohn did his work.

*

After death, Kelly's head
was cut off, shaved,
inspected by doctors.
A plaster cast was made.
The body was dissected.
Portions of the corpse
were displayed by Melbourne medical men
in 'curiosity cabinets'.
His skull was used as a paperweight
by a minor public official.

Bob Craig's Funeral

Organ music softly
crackles through tiny speakers
in this cut-price funeral chapel.
There aren't many people here
to send off Bob.
Down at the cycling club, Bobby
always made himself useful
as club masseur, fund raiser
and never had it away with anyone's missus.
But he'd never looked healthy.
Though a teetotaller,
diabetes got him at fifty.
His service was unremarkable
except when a hulking football star
with a head chiselled out of granite
came to the lectern then said,
'I knew Bob. He was my friend.'
And started to cry.

The Capture and Incarceration of Frank 'Captain Melville' McCallum (1822–1857)

Geelong, 1852:
Corio Street, the waterfront.
A brothel, Christmas Eve:
Frank McCallum,
with partner-in-crime,
Bill Roberts,
had been enjoying drink
and the company of women.
Roberts, blind drunk,
was sound asleep,
slumped upon a table.
McCallum remained more sober,
but didn't notice
one of the ladies
steal out a back door
while he held court.
(It was such exhausting work
robbing those travellers
on the Ballarat road,
he cheerfully bragged.)
She told the local police
who'd arrived in town,
tongue loosened by the prospect
of one hundred pounds reward.

Time passed… Frank sniffed trouble.
When he creaked the front door ajar,
preparing to escape
(Roberts being too drunk to follow),
he glimpsed two constables and a woman
walking towards the gate.
He grabbed a chair,
raced through the house,
shattered a rear window.
A leap into the twilight,
a shirt-front given to the constable
sent to cover the back.
Across vacant lots,
then Malop Street
a chased ensued
– McCallum and the three police.
Near La Trobe's Dam,
half a mile away,
he dragged a local man,
Henry Guy, off his horse.
But he couldn't mount the raring beast.
Indeed, Guy didn't know
with whom he was dealing
as he grappled with the desperate stranger
until the constables arrived.

Months later, Geelong Court:
Judge Redmond Barry presiding.
McCallum sentenced to thirty-two years
on charges of highway robbery,
term to be carried out
on prison hulks in Port Philip Bay.
He couldn't keep from trouble there
– attempting to bite off a sergeant's nose,
involved in an aborted escape
in which a constable, Owens,
had his head caved in with a hammer.
This time his sentence was death,
commuted to life
on a legal technicality.
'You'll be sorry for that,' McCallum warned.
The authorities were.
Transferred to Melbourne jail,
he stabbed its Governor, Wintle,
with a soup spoon sharpened into a shiv,
and was rumoured to have organised
the murder of John Price,
Superintendent of Victorian Prisons,
stoned to death by convicts
at Point Gellibrand quarry
in March 1857.

In the end, it seems,
McCallum was too much trouble.
Jail warders, most likely,
put him out of his misery,
though the coroner's jury returned the convenient
verdict of felo de se
– that he'd strangled himself in his cell.

Stringybark Creek

This is –
the iris of –
storm –

This is –
stark chill –
cold terror –

This is –
the thudding –
crimson heart –

Rifles poised –
in the speargrass –

Self-portrait with Death Playing the Fiddle

after Arnold Böcklin

The more I look
at what's ahead,
the more I sense
who's looming behind –
old fiddler Death
with a hideous laugh
playing me
to eternity.

Caspar David

Moon at dusk
– lambent, full,
filtered through ragged,
leaden clouds.
Man in foreground stands
upon a rugged peak.
He holds a walking-staff,
his back towards the viewer.
Gazing at velvet vastness,
streaky lunar yellow,
he almost touches heaven.

The Great War – AIF Suite

1. Captain Joseph Peter Lalor
(killed in action, Gallipoli, 25 April 1915)

Captain Joseph Peter Lalor,
the Eureka leader's grandson,
fought bravely,
dodged bullets for hours,
but then became unstrung.
He decided to charge,
stood up,
calling out to his men
not dead or wounded:
'Now then, Twelfth Battalion…'
A Turkish sniper's bullet
put a full stop
to his words,
his life.

2. Captain Alfred Shout, VC, MC
(died of wounds on HS *Neuralia*, Gallipoli, 11 August 1915)

'There's Shout,' he said.

'Where?'

'There,' he pointed.
'Having a joke,
as usual.
Puffing on a Woodbine,
as usual.'

'Looks like a good fella.'

'Irreplaceable,' he replied,
a tear running down his cheek,
pocketing the photograph.

3. Sergeant Jack Bubb
(Pozières, 23 July 1916)

Just after midnight the bombardment
was at its most intense.
But the expected word, to advance,
had not yet come.
Commotion and confusion.
Men were running back down the slope.
They thought there was an order to retreat.
Others yelled:
'Double back!
Double back!'
Was the day lost?
Were our hopes dashed?
Then came Jack Bubb,
swaggering and swearing,
scornful of all danger,
gathering his scattered men,
ordering them to once again
move forward to their places
(an order to retreat
had not been given).
He went up with them.
Soon I heard
his booming voice again:
'I'm all right! I'm all right!'
He was limping down the road, wounded,
supported by another.
Word came for machine-gunners.
Now my turn…

4. Squires
(killed in action, Pozières, 23 July 1916)

Now becoming daylight.
Got out of double dugout
shared with Steer,
left him to get some peace,
stretch out with his leg
– gaping gunshot wound, but bone not broken.
(I'd fixed it up
with field bandage
the best I could.)

Got in nearby hole
with unknown man.
This bloke,
I soon realised,
was dead.
Discovered by his ID discs
that it was Squires,
mate of Dunn's.
Been struck in head by shrapnel
while not wearing helmet.
Too tired to feel horror.
Fell fast asleep…

5. C. McK.
(killed in action, Pozières, probably 25 July 1916)

A shell exploded, demolishing
the corner of our trench.
I lost my helmet there
but in the crater found another.
It bore the initials 'C. McK.'
I put it on.

Sometime later, a pair of chaps,
noticing what was on my scone,
asked me if I knew
what had happened to Charlie.
Charlie McKnight, a mate of theirs,
had been gone for more than a day.
'Probably buried by a shell,'
was all that I could say.

6. Corporal Jagoe
(killed in action, Pozières, 25 July 1916)

Corporal Jagoe, forever smiling,
was always up for a lark or scrap.
But that last time, at Pozières,
his jaw was set, determined.
Fritz's bombs wreaked merry hell.
We lost touch. In the evening,
I saw his body on a path
in woods at the back of the town.
He was dead, unmarked,
as if asleep.
We who were left
had to hurry on.

7. Major Percy Black
(killed in action, First Bullecourt, 11 April 1917)

Percy Black, DSO, DCM, *Croix de Guerre*,
of the handlebar moustache,
chiselled jaw,
dark wavy hair
and barrel chest,
looked like the 'after' picture
in a Physical Culture magazine.
Lieutenant-Colonel
'Mad Harry' Murray,
the most decorated British Empire
infantry soldier in the Great War,
VC, DCM, DSO and Bar, *Croix de Guerre*,
thought Black, his best friend
(shot through the head
while leading his men
through razor wire at First Bellecourt),
'the bravest man in the A.I.F'.

With his bravery, Percy was gentle,
drily humorous too.
On leave in London, in 1916,
he was almost hit by a bus.
After he reached the kerb, he quipped
that he'd like to rejoin his mates at the front
'because a man's not safe over here'.

8. Captain Knox, 13th Australian Artillery Field Brigade

(killed in action, Menin Road, 17 August 1917)

Bill was clever and witty,
like many others anxious
not to worry his family.
So his letters home were woven
with amusing anecdotes,
comic reflections on Turks or Fritz,
generous words when he thought they fought well,
and assurances that he was safe.
This went on for years,
from Gallipoli through to Menin Road.
Then that gas attack.
Then the letters stopped.

Forever.

www.ingramcontent.com/pod-product-compliance
Lightning Source LLC
Chambersburg PA
CBHW062156100526
44589CB00014B/1853